MASSAGE AT YOUR FINGERTIPS

Explains in non-technical language how to perform the principal massage movements for the renewal and invigoration of the whole body.

MASSAGE AT YOUR FINGERTIPS

Prepared and produced by the Editorial Committee of Science of Life Books

Revised by E.R. Triance D.O., M.C.O., L.S.P.O.
Osteopath and Physiatrician

SCIENCE OF LIFE BOOKS
4-12 Tattersalls Lane, Melbourne, Victoria 3000

First published in this series 1974
Second Edition, revised and reset, 1984
Second Impression 1986

National Library of Australia card number and
ISBN 0 909911 09 6

Printed in Great Britain by
Richard Clay Ltd, Bungay, Suffolk

Contents

Preface

Here is a simple guide to the 'Father of All Healing'. As far back as 400 BC the great Hippocrates employed massage and manipulation in treating his patients. Since that early period massage has been the means of treating many ailments and of restoring sufferers to health and vigour.

We all want to assist our sick and ailing friends, and here in simple terms are set forth the methods by which the flow of blood and lymph may be quickened, the function of the skin improved and nutrition increased.

Here, in brief, are explained the means by which the whole physical form may be renewed and invigorated.

1

Massage as an Aid to Health

In spite of the development of sophisticated equipment for the treatment of physical injury, and the wide range of electrical apparatus that has replaced the use of massage in physical therapy, it is perhaps surprising to find that effective and quick relief is so often brought about by massage alone when all other treatments have failed. Proper and judicious use of massage techniques will continue to be of value for as long as there are those prepared to practise them.

Although masseurs survive predominantly in association with sports and athletic clubs where their work is most notably recognized it would be sad if massage were to be neglected as a method of treatment for all the general disorders it can undoubtedly assist.

It is indisputable that the human body functions much more efficiently when it is not structurally restricted, and the modern way of life clearly induces tight muscles, stiff joints, tense personalities and stressed organs, all of which could respond to and in many cases be completely alleviated by massage, a valuable agent for the improvement of physical and mental well-being.

If we wish to practice massage we must be discerning in our application of it.

Care and Judgement

Care and judgment are required; for no two persons or natures are quite alike. Each one calls for *special* treatment; not only because of differences in outward physical features, but also because of contrasts in temperament and disposition.

We must take into consideration the *whole make-up* of each individual patient. Not only must the condition of the skin and soft tissues be carefully noted, but also the nervous system and mental state.

One person may need, and benefit from, vigorous treatment, while another might resent the least suspicion of over forceful or unsympathetic handling.

Indeed, it may be said that in many cases patients know their particular needs, and will resent any treatment that seems to them to be unsuitable. This applies to a marked degree in cases of neurasthenia or nervous debility. Such patients are intensely sensitive and extremely quick in their reactions.

There are, however, many cases in which patients are as reserved as they are sensitive. They fail to express any disapproval of the treatment they receive, and consequently may give up treatment.

Insight and Intuition

It is important to establish some rapport with all patients because the success of the treatment may depend in the first instance upon the ability of the masseur to gain the patient's trust and respect. Even the most effective physical treatment will not be wholly successful without the confidence of the patient.

A person having natural insight and intuition will be more likely to succeed as a masseur or masseuse. Both men and women are equally suited to practise massage. It is not only necessary to be gentle and sympathetic but also have a firm grasp with an ability to apply deep pressure with the fingers. The work can be demanding but great strength is not essential and strength in the wrist and fingers will automatically develop from continued practice. There have been very successful practitioners of small build as well as of big and heavy build.

The work requires sympathetic consideration of the finer feelings of the patient.

It is, however, natural that highly-trained and business-like operators should desire to get on with their work without any 'bother or nonsense'. Their treatment is, no doubt, admirable as regards technique and approved methods, but the fact remains that patients resent being treated as though they were rubber dolls, made to a set pattern.

In certain hospitals patients may, owing to pressure of work, be compelled to submit at times to what has been termed 'mass treatment'.

Private patients, however, expect to be treated as distinct personalities, and to be shown the nicest regard for their feelings. Indeed, the pleasing and sympathetic bedside manner, which is deemed so important in a doctor of medicine, is of equal, if not greater, value in a masseur or masseuse.

He or she, by the ease of their approach, should be able to dispel all shyness and nervousness, and thus be in a position to treat patients as naturally as a nurse treats a child.

A High Ideal

It is a high ideal; but the fact remains that in general massage, which calls for the manipulation of the whole of the soft tissues, there must be childish submission to the 'healing hands', and both the patient and the operator must feel that the treatment is as natural as the daily round of the nursery.

Even so, it may be that human feelings will be aroused; but in the great majority of cases the reactions will be so gentle and pleasant as to be distinctly beneficial. This will apply to a marked degree when patients are making a slow, painful and lonely recovery from a long illness.

In such cases the human touch may have a magical effect in the restoration of health. We must, therefore, apply ourselves to this healing work, and learn to use our hands so that they will follow the guidance of our judgment and tact. There are many cases in which we may render beneficial help, if we aim at treating the human form as thoughtfully and carefully as we are advised to treat the human spirit.

2

Skill with the Hands

The leading massage movements are known as *effleurage, pétrissage, friction* and *tapotement*.

In general massage, dealing with the whole body, each and all of the movements would probably be employed, in conjunction with other movements of peculiar interest and importance. But before we dwell upon them in detail we must refresh our minds with regard to the main aim and purpose of massage.

Broadly speaking, the aim of modern scientific massage is to restore the normal condition of the body.

We must, therefore, be intent upon benefiting all the parts to which our work is directed — the skin, the muscles, the blood vessels, the lymphatics and, moreover, the whole nervous system.

At the same time we must aim at aiding digestion, absorption and assimilation.

If our work is skilfully done, we shall find that we have stimulated the nutrition of the areas we have treated by bringing a fresh flow of blood to them, and causing an interchange of fluid within the tissues.

Later, we shall see how massage can remove and prevent the formation of adhesions after bodily injury, and how it can remove inflammation and swellings and disperse congestion.

Moreover, we shall deal with the work which may be done, under medical supervision, in dislocations and fractures.

Muscles and Joints

In such work a knowledge of anatomy is, of course, of great value, particularly when combined with sound judgment and natural skill with the hands.

Indeed, it may be said that unless the would-be operator has the healing sense, and delicacy of touch, the widest knowledge of the subject will be of little or no avail.

The masseur who relies simply on his natural skill, and seeks medical advice in time of need, may, therefore, hope to do very helpful and beneficial work.

He will, however, be easier in his mind and have greater self-assurance if he has knowledge of the position of the muscles of the body and the functioning of joints, etc. Fortunately, our own physical forms and many books are available to aid in such study.

'Know thyself' is a very good maxim for the would-be masseur — know every part of the body. The Latin names of the muscles, which are so numerous and so hard to remember, are of small account compared with the valuable gift of recognizing the tissues and their condition by sensitive and intelligent touch.

A good plan is to make anatomical sketches of the muscles and joints, etc. In this way they are, so to speak, fixed in the mind's eye, and will not be readily forgotten.

If the knowledge thus gained leads to closer and deeper study, so much the better; and if it tends to encourage interest in physiology as well as anatomy the student will be on the way to becoming a well-qualified masseur.

If his enthusiasm leads him to enter a school of massage, or take up a correspondence course, he will nevertheless, find that in addition to book learning he must acquire a high degree of skill with his hands.

To have brains in the fingertips is good, but not

enough. There must, so to speak, be brains in every part of the hands, so that they will know by touch the condition of the soft tissues and be able to manipulate them in accordance with their need.

This is not so difficult as it may seem. Every man and woman of average intelligence and skill can develop the latent sensitiveness and agility of their hands, as witness the amazing dexterity displayed by jugglers.

Exercising the Hands

It is largely a matter of practice. We should regularly exercise our hands, strengthen them with the use of hand grips and take every opportunity of increasing manual dexterity. The playing of musical instruments is, of course, an aid to intelligent use of the hands. For those who do not play an instrument any method of becoming adept, not only with the fingers but also with the palms and wrists, should be used.

A simple cushion or pillow, if it were filled, can be used to develop the power and skill of the hands required in some massage movements such as stroking and kneading.

Nothing, however, can be a substitute for the real thing and every opportunity should be sought to practise the movements on a human model or, better still, on as many different subjects as possible. The great advantage is that they will be able to say what the treatment feels like and whether it is successfully stimulating or relaxing them and also if the aim of the movements is being achieved.

The aim is simple — delicacy or firmness of touch, as the need arises, and the ability to glide easily from one movement to another.

Each case treated will give greater skill and increased confidence, until the hands of the operator become, in the true sense, *healing hands*.

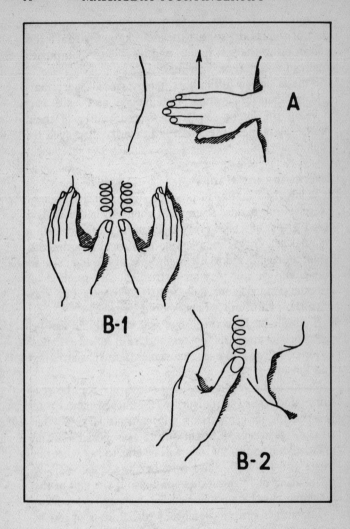

Leading massage movements. A — Effleurage. B-1 and
B-2 — Friction.

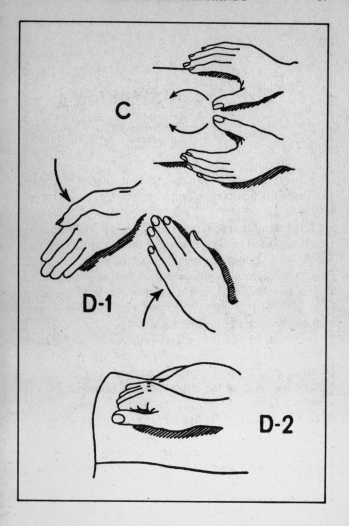

Leading massage movements. C — Petrissage. D-1 and
D-2 — Tapotement.

3

The Art of Stroking

We may now dwell upon the first of the massage movements, which is known as effleurage, pronounced *ef-fler-arje*.

This has the appearance of being a very simple movement and easily performed; for it mainly consists of stroking. But in the present case the word, *stroking,* has a special meaning and calls for skill and judgment.

Just to stroke without the correct degree of pressure and without thought to direction and purpose would fail to produce the desired result.

Our aim, in the first place, must be to soothe the nerves and induce relaxation. With this aim in view all massage begins and frequently ends.

The direction of the stroke should, traditionally, be upward, towards the heart, and in the course of the blood vessels and lymphatics. Our touch should be in soothing contact with the part undergoing treatment.

We shall see later that this opening movement, together with deep breathing, is of particular importance in *general* massage, in the treatment, that is, of the whole body.

The Right Leg
For the moment, we will direct our attention to one limb, and take, for example, the right leg.

Having given carefully the first soothing

movements, we may work with firmer pressure, and thus encourage the flow of the venous blood and lymph.

The extremity of the limb — or, more correctly, just above the ankle — should be held with one hand, while the other hand presses firmly and smoothly upward, with the palms and the fingers moulded to the tissues beneath.

The movement should be repeated several times, beginning in each case at the distal end of the limb and ending near the groin.

The moving hand will, or course, be raised or relaxed at the knee joint.

The Right Arm

Now take the right arm, with the view to giving it similar effleurage treatment. In this case the patient's hand should be held firmly, and the upward movement of the operator's other hand should end at the armpit, allowance being made, of course, for the elbow joint.

Both the operator's hands should be used when giving effleurage treatment to such parts of the trunk as the abdomen and the back; for these are large areas, allowing broad treatment.

The same care should, however, be exercised. The first few strokes should be of a soothing character, and the pressure increased as the work continues.

Further suggestions with regard to these large areas will be given in the chapter dealing with *general* massage.

We have dwelt on the art of stroking the limbs with one hand. It is possible, however, that some limbs needing treatment may be so wide in girth as to require the use of both hands, particularly as regards the thighs. In such cases, both the operator's hands will

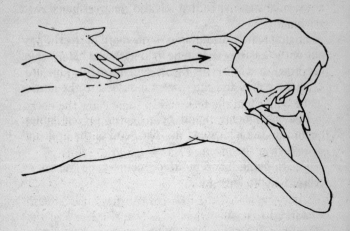

Direction of strokes in effleurage of long back muscles.

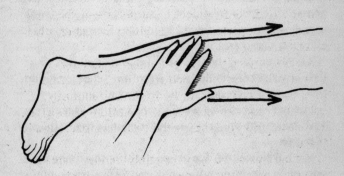

Direction of strokes in effleurage of lower leg.

encircle the limb under treatment, and move upward in a similar manner to that advised for treatment with one hand.

For small areas, stroking with the 'ball' of the thumb and with the fingertips may be employed. Here also the pressure will be light at first, and then gradually increased.

The hands and the feet, and in some cases the neck, may be treated with the 'ball' of the thumb, while the tips of the fingers may be used in the treatment of the patient's fingers and toes and around the joints.

Unhealthy Conditions

It is important that the masseur, or masseuse, should be assured that all patients are free from any of the unhealthy conditions that make massage treatment definitely inadvisable. At the back of the book will be found names of the conditions in which massage should *not* be given. It is more than likely that sufferers from the ailments mentioned will be under the care of a doctor, who will naturally guard them from harm.

In any case, medical advice should be sought when there is any doubt as to the suitability of patients for massage treatment.

Our aim is to help the large number of sufferers who can derive nothing but good from our work. Among these, as we have seen, are many persons enduring, as best they can, the distressing condition known as nervous debility, and the general weakness that follows long illness.

In such cases we may certainly render valuable assistance, providing we exercise the care advocated in Chapter 1.

Other conditions will call for special local treatment and the employment of special means. But these, as we shall see later, may also be treated with every hope of success.

4

Persuasive Treatment

The next of the leading massage movements calls for what has been termed 'persuasive treatments'. It is known as pétrissage and includes a movement of considerable importance, called kneading, with which we will deal later in this chapter.

'Essence' of Modern Massage

Our aim for the moment is to examine broadly what is involved in pétrissage and to show how it is, in a sense, the 'essence' of modern massage. It may, indeed, be said that in the various forms of pétrissage the operator's powers of manipulation are revealed at their true value.

The skilful masseur will give a few soothing movements to the area under treatment and then pick up the smaller muscles between his thumb and forefingers, and so manipulate them that they gain new vitality.

Sensitive hands will readily trace the formation of the muscles, and will feel their response to treatment.

The hands may be used in various ways, according to the locality of the muscles. When dealing with the limbs both hands may be gradually moved upward in a series of manipulative movements, commonly known as 'squeezing'.

Care must, however, be taken not to bruise or injure

the tissues. If in the place of 'squeezing', we aim rather at rolling the muscles we shall be in a safer position.

In all pétrissage, particularly rolling and kneading, it is important that the work should be done slowly and continued patiently until the desired effect is obtained.

For small muscles one hand may suffice for the work, while in restricted areas, the operator's fingers may be all that can be employed. This will be the case when dealing with tissues in close proximity to joints.

Kneading

By what means the larger muscles are raised and treated rests mainly with the individual operator. Some masseurs as we have seen, think of it as 'squeezing', others as 'grasping', and others as 'pinching'. But no such terms are quite satisfactory. Indeed, it would seem that new words are needed to describe the precise character of the work.

It is, however, simple in character, and may be thought of in association with the homely word, *kneading*.

Every part of the hands should, where possible, be used when giving *kneading* treatment. The fingers, the thumbs and the palms of the hands should embrace the larger muscles, coaxing them into movement, and thus renewing their vitality.

The degree of pressure will be dictated by the nature and condition of the tissues. In some cases the so-called 'grasp' will be more like a gentle embrace. In other cases the muscles may permit, and benefit from, a definite, yet cautious, use of pressure.

A clever cook, kneading dough, might be taken as an illustration of the kind of work required. But it must be remembered that a masseur or masseuse deals with *living* tissues.

The action of wringing or twisting the larger

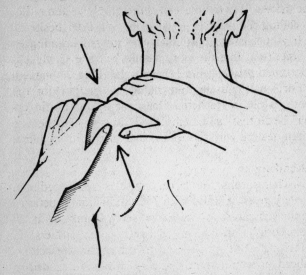

Position for kneading shoulder with both hands.

muscles is also included in pétrissage. In this method the muscle is taken into the operator's hands and turned on the bone, both hands moving in the same direction, which is then reversed.

The muscles of the limbs may be treated in this way, the tissues being turned on the bone. Care should, of course, be taken not to use too great a degree of pressure; and 'jerking' movements must be carefully avoided.

The aim, it must be remembered, is to give the muscles new life and vigour. Other methods of achieving the desired result may present themselves, and may be adopted; for in massage there are no absolutely hard and fast rules.

Massage is not a mechanical process. It is work in which individual powers of judgment and touch may be employed.

It is advisable first to master the primary methods and movements. It is particularly important that the student should study the art of *kneading* the muscles, and make every effort to develop touch so as to be able to tell precisely what is required, and be in a position to give the treatment most likely to benefit the patient.

5

Treating the Underlying Tissues

The muscles, as we have observed, are placed upon the body in layers, one upon another. Our aim now is to treat the lower muscles, and for this purpose we employ the movement known as *friction*.

Circular Movements

Firstly, we place the tips of our fingers or our thumbs on the part to be treated. We then move the tissues beneath the surface with circular movements, taking care meanwhile to maintain the pressure, and to avoid the error of allowing our fingers or thumbs to glide over the surface.

We may practise on various parts of our own body, pressing as advised, and with circular movement stimulating the lower tissues.

The treatment should be in *small* circles, and should be repeated as we progress in an upward direction, raising our fingers or thumbs to gain a higher area, or, for the moment, allowing them to glide.

Deep pressure may often be required, so that the upper tissues may be pressed on those beneath, or on to a bone. Care should be taken not to be unduly forceful.

The treatment is of special value when dealing with the flat muscles, which cannot be taken into the hands and kneaded. It is also helpful in treating the spine,

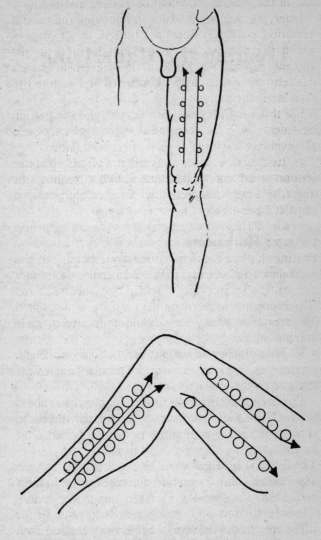

Direction of friction movements to long muscles of the leg, using both thumbs.

and in the general treatment of tendons and joints.

Later, we shall see its value in removing the painful condition known as fibrositis. Indeed, in all cases in which the muscles are 'gritty' and hard, as in the ailment named, we have in the movement means whereby the tissues may be softened and restored to their normal condition.

For this work pressure will be used, and the friction treatment will be continued with patience and perseverance until the desired effect is obtained.

In treating the spine it is often advisable to give friction treatment in close proximity to each of the joints, dealing with both sides with carefully placed circular movements.

In a later chapter, dealing with massage of the whole body, we shall see that friction is not only helpful in treating the localities and conditions named, but also in dealing with the neck, face and head.

The Neck
The treatment of the neck should be in circles, again designed to reach the lower tissues. Both the thumbs may be employed together, or in turn, while the fingers lightly grasp the neck. The direction of the circles will again be upward, towards the jawbone.

This treatment will, of course, be given mainly to the back and sides of the neck, and it will be found very helpful in cases of stiffness.

The Throat and Face
The throat and face call for delicate handling, particularly the throat.

Gentle friction and gentle pétrissage and gentle effleurage may, however, be given to the face, beginning with light stroking to relax the muscles.

Here the operator will enjoy the opportunity of

exercising delicacy of touch, and demonstrating how gentleness may be an expression of reserved power.

In treating the head with friction the movement will again be in the form of small circles, and the aim will be to move the scalp on the bone, and thus cause a fresh flow of blood.

The tapotement treatment, which may also be given to the scalp and very lightly to the face, will be described in the next chapter.

It is important to remember that in giving friction treatment the skin is moved in small circles in such a way as to affect the underlying tissues. In no circumstances must we, while actually employing the movement, allow our fingers or thumbs to glide over the skin.

6

Stimulating Movements

We have seen how massage movements have been devised to influence the tissues in various ways. Indeed, it may be said that there is scarcely any limit to the means that may be employed by skilful and ingenious operators in seeking to obtain the desired effect.

The movements we have dealt with have been carefully contrived with the view to obtaining clear and definite results, and to act as a general guide in giving massage treatment. It was never intended, however, that they should be followed absolutely and 'to the letter'.

No two operators are quite alike in nature and temperament, just as surely as no two patients are quite alike. The masseur will use his hands in the manner dictated by his own nature. He may, in a sense, follow the set formulas; but it will be in his own way, just as any expert performs with his own particular interpretation.

We may take it that the various forms of the treatment known as tapotement — pronounced *ta-pot-mon* — will be performed in various ways, particularly when we take into account that all movements of a vibratory character come under the same general heading.

The most important and the most frequently

practised are the movements known as tapping, hacking, beating or drumming, shaking, boating and digital vibrations.

Tapping

The first — tapping — is one of the methods advised for treating the head, and, very gently, the face. The operator's hands are held in much the same manner as those of a person playing the piano. The fingers are rapidly lowered from the wrists in a series of tapping movements, thus stimulating the parts under treatment.

Punctuation is another name given to this method of increasing the blood–supply and stimulating the muscle tissue. It is claimed, moreover, that it lessens nerve irritability. But such results can only be obtained if the tapping is correctly given, the fingers leaving the surface after each stroke and then rapidly returned.

Hacking

Hacking is another important form of tapotement. In this movement the edges of the hands are brought down in short, rapid, alternative strokes, first one hand, then the other, coming into sharp (but not violent) contact with the muscles.

A similar stimulating effect may be obtained by the treatment known as beating or drumming. In this movement the hands are lightly closed, and then brought down from the wrists in stimulating contact with the tissues under treatment.

The two movements — hacking and beating — are helpful in treating the larger muscles of limbs, and, in particular, the lumbar muscles and buttocks.

Shaking

Shaking is another method used at times in treating the

limbs. In this treatment the limb is held firmly and
shaken in a manner designed to give freedom of action
and restore normal conditions.

Cupping

In the movement known as cupping the operator's
hand is relaxed and partly closed so as to form a
'pillow' of air when it is brought into rapid contact
with the tissues.

Vibration

In cases of nerve pain, such as suffered in sciatica, it is
frequently found that the movement known as
vibration will give relief. In this treatment the middle
fingers (or the large fingers only) are placed on the
painful localities, and very rapidly, yet lightly,
vibrated.

With these tapotement movements at our command,
together with the movements already described, we
can now consider what is required in the treatment of
the body as a whole, known as *general massage*.

7

General Massage

Here we emphasize afresh the need for intimate knowledge of the human form. But we have seen that there are equally important needs, such as judgment, skill and tact. The widest knowledge of anatomy would not compensate for lack of skill in carrying out the practical side of our work.

Beginners need not, therefore, be disheartened. Let them study their own bodies, the formation of the muscles, the working of the joints and the functioning of the internal organs. In this way they will gain knowledge of a kind that book learning might fail to supply.

Individual Treatment
We cannot dwell too often on such advice, or upon the oft-repeated injunction that each patient must be given individual treatment. Many operators have failed to give satisfaction because they have thought almost entirely of themselves and their work, and omitted to take into thoughtful consideration the patient's nature and his, or her, reactions to massage treatment.

This important matter is raised again because we intend to give massage to the whole physical form, and so have in view work which will affect the patient's whole being.

Preparation

In the first place we must be sure that the unclothed patient is resting quite comfortably in bed, with the blankets, etc., so arranged that they may be turned back as we proceed to treat the various parts of the body. An extra blanket may prove helpful, but is not absolutely necessary.

There are divisions of opinion with regard to the use of talcum powder and lubricants but these should be available. A lubricant would be used if there is any indication of local roughness or tenderness of the skin. A good talcum powder may be put to general use, and is often found to be a source of comfort to the patient.

The operator's hands should be washed in warm water, and his wrists should be free from the encumbrance of coat sleeves, etc. His manner should be self-reliant and confident, yet gentle and sympathetic, particularly when dealing with patients of sensitive disposition.

On approaching the bed, he may, if he thinks it advisable, take the patient's pulse in the usual way, remembering that the normal in an adult is 72 beats a minute.

He will then request his patient to breathe slowly and deeply several times, and will see that this is done in a way that causes a sense of composure and induces relaxation.

Treatment of Limbs

Having decided in his mind the degree of energy he may exercise in performing the various massage movements, the operator will begin with the left arm, and give effleurage treatment from the wrist to the elbow, and from the elbow to the shoulder. Pétrissage, with kneading, will follow, and possibly friction. Then again the masseur will employ gentle stroking treatment, and will give assisted movements to the joints of the limb he has treated.

He will then treat the left leg in a similar manner — effleurage, pétrissage, with kneading, and possibly friction in the locality of the joints, concluding with stroking treatment and assisted movements.

He will then go to the opposite side of the bed and treat the right arm and leg in the manner prescribed for the limbs on the left side.

Chest and Abdomen
Having completed the treatment of the limbs, he will give his attention to the chest and the abdomen.

The treatment of the chest will vary according to the physical structure of the patient. Effleurage and light friction may, however, be given in the majority of cases.

Massage of the abdomen is more exacting, particularly when giving treatment for chronic constipation, with which we deal in a later chapter.

Sequence of Movements
In general treatment, it is the custom to begin with effleurage in the form of soothing movements over the whole surface of the abdomen, thus causing relaxation of the tissues. Friction may then be given in a clockwise course, starting with the outer area and continuing in small circles to the centre. Kneading movements may follow, or be given earlier. In many cases, the treatment should again conclude with effleurage.

The patient should then turn to a prone position — face downward — and thus be in a position for treatment of the back and loins and the posterior thighs.

The prescribed movements should be given —

effleurage, pétrissage, friction, tapotement — to each area, with special friction treatment to the spine, the fingers resting firmly, while moving in small circles in close proximity to the spinal column.

For the larger flat muscles of the back, both hands may be used in wide circular kneading, and tapotement may follow. This treatment would, however, be preceded by effleurage over the whole area of the back, and would conclude with the same movement given with firm yet soothing strokes.

The lumbar muscles and the soft tissues of the loins and the backs of the thighs should then be given effleurage, followed by pétrissage, mainly in the form of kneading.

Again, the treatment should conclude with effleurage in the form of soothing strokes over the whole area.

Risk of Fatigue

The actual time taken in the work will depend upon the condition and nature of the patient. But in all circumstances it is advisable not to run the risk of fatigue. Detailed treatment to the hands and feet, etc., may, if thought advisable, be postponed.

Care should be taken throughout the whole treatment to keep the patient warm. Only the parts under actual treatment should be exposed, and these should be covered as soon as possible.

Providing the work has been done with skill and discretion, the hands of the operator gliding smoothly from movement to movement, the patient will enjoy a sense of well-being and be prepared for restful sleep.

8

First Aid for Convalescents

In the weakness and debility following illness, massage may render most valuable service.

It is, however, important that we should keep in mind the condition of the patient, not only the condition of the bodily tissues, but also the mental and nervous state.

We should think of ourselves as giving, so to speak, 'first aid' and of rendering 'relief service' in preparation for further good work later.

It may be that the treatment we consider advisable will not take more than, say, ten minutes. But it will, if we are wise, be of a nature that soothes and comforts, and prepares the way for further and deeper massage.

Our effleurage strokes will, at first, be of the gentlest character, and if we add kneading that, too, will be given so as to have a soothing and comforting effect.

We may, in the first place, ask the patient to breathe slowly and rather deeply, but without marked effort.

It will rest with our own judgment to decide what part of the body to massage first. Some convalescent patients prefer to have the main part of the treatment given to the back, where long, rhythmic strokes may be given slowly and gently over the full length of the spine, one hand following the other.

The 'Human Touch'

Much has been written in a poetical and romantic sense about the remarkable value of the 'human touch' in social relationships. Well, here we may speak of the human touch in a literal sense, the actual touch, that is, of the human hand, with all its healing powers.

We are imagining that it is our privilege to help back to health and vigour a friend who has had a long and painful illness, and as a result, is weak and listless.

Following the deep but easy breathing and the soothing effleurage strokes and the gentle kneading of the back, we shall continue the treatment, if advisable, over the loins and back of the thighs and the calves, thus strengthening the muscles that help to support the back, and giving new vitality to the lower limbs.

We may also treat the back of the neck with gentle effleurage and kneading, thus helping muscles that are often weak and painful after long illness.

Effleurage may then be given afresh to the whole area we have covered. If given slowly, gently and smoothly the treatment will induce a pleasant sleepiness, and may well end the treatment for the first day.

In any case, care must be taken not to exhaust or in any way 'try' the patient. It is better to do too little than too much.

The aim, at first, will be to exercise the human touch in the manner suggested, and so prepare the way for the whole body to be treated later.

Keeping the Patient Warm

We dwelt in the previous chapter on the advisability of keeping the patient warm, and of covering each part immediately after treatment, and of the operator washing his, or her, hands in warm water, and of the use of talcum powder, etc.

The primary aim must be to leave the patient warm and soothed and comfortable, and in a fit condition to enjoy restful slumber. But it may be that in convalescence a suitable time, if not the best, for giving treatment will be shortly after the patient's morning toilet, when the effect of suitable massage will be to strengthen the physical frame and give a new sense of life to the patient.

If further treatment is given in the evening, it should follow the course advised, and end with movements of a distinctly soothing character.

9

Treatment for
Lower Back Strain

Friends may also play a helpful part in dealing with the common, but very painful complaint known as lower back strain. The massage, however, will be of a different character from the gentle treatment advised in the previous chapter.

Here the operator will need to go much deeper; for lower back strain is due to inflammation of the fibrous sheaths of the lumbar muscles. To reach this inflamed condition the masseur will need to exercise a very considerable, though cautious, degree of pressure.

We all know how distressing lower back strain can be, and how the least movement can cause intense pain. The operator will, therefore, have to exercise great care and patience in getting the sufferer into the right position for massage treatment.

The patient will, of course, have to turn, or be turned, to a prone position — face downward — and it will be a comfort to him, and also a help to the masseur, if a pillow is placed under the abdomen.

With this support the masseur will be able to employ the necessary degree of pressure in giving friction and pétrissage, also kneading and tapotement.

The Lumbar Muscles
He will, however, commence the treatment with effleurage strokes over the upper part of the loins; for

here are the lumbar muscles that are the main causes of the trouble.

In the ordinary course of a sedentary life these muscles are seldom brought into active use. Consequently they are subject to a painful condition from which muscles in frequent use rarely suffer. A cold wind, an unusual movement, causing strain, and other reasons, will have the effect of causing the painful state that is only too familiar.

Fortunately, however, lower back strain is not in itself a very serious condition, though sufferers may experience very acute pain. It is most important to establish that the patient does not have a 'slipped disc' or other spinal lesion because of the danger of aggravating the symptoms by wrong treatment. Although massage can be of assistance, properly applied, in such cases and is certainly very beneficial in rehabilitation after such injuries and, on the whole, much more beneficial than many electrical treatments.

Having soothed the patient with stroking movements, designed to bring about a relaxed condition of the painful muscles, the next aim will be to soften the fibrous tissues with deep friction over the whole of the affected area.

The operator's fingers must be placed firmly on the skin and held in close contact while they are moved in small circles in such a manner as to reach the underlying tissues. Having treated one small section, the masseur's fingers will move to the next area, and so on, until the whole of the lumbar muscles have been treated.

Pétrissage will follow, the offending muscles being raised and 'rolled', and then given firm kneading. Care will, of course, be taken not to exercise too much vigour. The patient will, no doubt, quickly protest if unbearable pain is caused.

The treatment should, however, have the effect of softening the offending fibres, and so removing the cause of the trouble.

Tapotement movements will next be given, in the form of light but effective 'beating' with the half-clenched hand. This will be followed by 'hacking' treatment, performed with the outward edges of the operator's hands, moving from his wrists in sharp alternative strokes.

The treatment will continue for some time, and should be repeated until the patient has recovered, and even afterwards, thus lessening any fear of a return of the trouble.

Other aids to recovery, such as placing a hot-water bottle close to the affected muscles may be suggested; but there is little doubt that every friend who visits the sufferer will know, or will have heard, of some so-called cure, and the use of heat will, no doubt, be among the suggested remedies.

In any case, it is important that the patient should be kept warm, both during massage treatment and after.

No time should be lost in dealing with the trouble; for lower back strain, if neglected, may lead to the greater pains and penalties of sciatica (with which we will deal in the next chapter).

When such a condition arises specialist aid will, no doubt, be sought, and appropriate manipulative movements given by a trained manipulator. Massage treatment for lower back strain will be frequent and prolonged, and may be accompanied by exercises designed to restore the normal condition of the affected muscles.

Patience and perseverance will be demanded. But it may be found, in due course, that with the faithful co-operation of his patient, a skilful operator can bring about a cure that may seem like a miracle.

10

Treatment for Sciatica

Sciatica has been described as neuralgia of the large nerve of the thigh, known as the sciatic nerve. The description is far from adequate.

Pressure within the deep muscles of the pelvis on the sciatic nerve is very often the cause of the trouble but by no means the only cause. This may result in inflammation of the nerve causing extreme pain to radiate down the whole course of the nerve and in such circumstances can be assisted by deep treatment of the structures adjacent to the nerve itself.

However, sciatica frequently is only a symptom arising in consequence of another condition; a prolapsed disc, arthritis of the spine, arthritis of the hip being examples. Less commonly it may result from disease of the bowels, liver or kidneys for example. Careful enquiry should be made about medical history and if no medical diagnosis has been made medical examination is advisable.

Help may be given in cases of nerve compression with deep treatment of the muscles and joints adjacent to painful areas and with patience a considerable amount of success achieved. Where the sciatica arises from other disorders palliative treatment can still be given and bring a measure of relief.

In the past it was generally believed that very deep pressure into the head of the nerve in the buttocks was the effective treatment to reduce inflammation of the nerve. It is now accepted that direct deep massage of the nerve does not reduce inflammation but that the inflammation will diminish when the muscles and tissues creating the pressure are relaxed.

Soothing Strokes

But the amateur will be wise if he notes carefully the origin and source of the trouble, and begins his treatment with effleurage in long soothing strokes down the full length of the nerve.

Carefully administered friction may follow, but the main part of this treatment will be given to the buttock in which the head of the nerve is set. Here the pressure may be as deep as the patient can endure but avoiding the inflamed nerve itself.

If pain is caused, it may be taken as an indication that the inflammation has been located, and it is now left to the skill of the operator to devise means whereby the surrounding fibres may be freed from unhealthy 'stringiness' and restored to a normal condition.

Increasing pressure will be required and the experienced operator may venture to use both hands, one reinforcing the other. But if pain persists after the treatment, it must be taken as a sign that the patient is not in a fit condition to endure deep friction.

Effleurage of a definitely soothing character should follow all friction treatment.

When the condition of the patient improves he may be advised to place one hand firmly on his kneecap and the other hand under the joint, and then raise the leg as far as he is able without causing great pain, thereby stretching the nerve.

Another method of 'stretching' the nerve is by bending the knee and drawing the whole limb back on to the abdomen. This simple but effective movement may be performed by the patient, who will know how much pressure he can bear.

Indeed, the patient must guide the operator in every stage of the treatment. Only by observing the patient's reactions and noting any indication of acute pain is it possible to give relief and bring about an ultimate cure.

Effleurage treatment will then be given once more, not only to the buttock, but also the thigh and calf and the whole length of the leg.

Certain medical lubricants, containing capsicum in some cases, have been considered a source of temporary relief. But it cannot be said that they remove the cause of the trouble.

It may, however, be taken that the first aim must be to give the patient freedom from pain. The masseur, is therefore, given an opportunity of showing how a light yet sure touch may disperse unhealthy conditions, and not simply give relief from pain, but eventually bring about a cure.

Sciatic pain has been indentified by Consultant Physicians as being a symptom of toxic conditions in the bloodstream caused by such practices as over indulgence in alcohol or cigarettes, or disorder of the organs. In these cases general massage may very well be beneficial.

11

Treatment for
Rheumatism and Arthritis

The words rheumatic and rheumatism are frequently very broadly used, and are spoken of in association with a very wide range of ailments, some light and temporary, others intense and persistent.

We know only too well how, as the years advance, muscles and joints become the prey of unhealthy conditions and cause pain, even when the sufferer is warm and snug in bed. And it may be that, owing to lowered vitality and powers of resistance, the pain will continue throughout the day, and the sufferer will be advised to try this, that, and the other so-called remedy.

The remarkable fact is that such so-called remedies, provided there is sufficient faith in them, do, in a sense, give relief, simply because they raise the spirits and the vitality of sufferers.

We have in mind the persons who in the ordinary course enjoy good health and freedom from rheumatism, yet become victims of pain, as a result of a run-down and depressed condition.

Maintain your vitality is, therefore, a golden rule for the avoidance of the first symptoms of the painful complaint. *Be on your guard!*

It is, of course, at such a time that massage, by maintaining the free flow of blood and lymph and a healthy condition of muscle and bone, can be of great value.

Aids to Vitality

General massage should be given, with special attention to any parts that threaten to cause pain. It will also aid in maintaining vitality if the patient follows a course of deep breathing and other physical exercises.

We all know the main rules of health, and need rather the will and determination to follow them than detailed instructions. It seems, however, that there are some people who fail to realize the great importance of keeping the bowels free from the least suspicion of poisonous matter.

Here, again, massage may be of great value, and in the next chapter we shall see that there are special ways and means of relieving constipation.

Our aim here must be to deal, so far as space permits, with actual rheumatic conditions, particularly with unhealthy and painful muscles.

All the leading massage movements are employed in such cases, and other movements may be devised by the masseur to combat the particular condition under treatment.

The operator, as intimated, is free to exercise his own particular gifts. It will be found, however, that pétrissage, combined with kneading and deep friction, will achieve very good results. Other leading movements, falling under the general heading, tapotement, such as 'beating', as described, will also help to bring about the desired result.

The aim is, of course, to reduce inflammation and soften the fibrous tissues.

Arthritis

When we come to the various forms of arthritis we are confronted by far more difficult conditions, for the dread word indicates inflammation of joints, which may be due, as in rheumatoid arthritis, to infection, or to injury, as in traumatic arthritis.

Not all arthritis sufferers are affected alike. In some cases the pain may be unbearable while in others only discomfort or numbness indicates that the disease is yet in its earlier stages of development. Usually the pains and deformities develop gradually but occasionally the onset may be sudden. Sometimes the disorder is limited to one joint while in other cases a number of joints or even the whole body is affected.

Those who suffer from limited degrees of the complaint should bear in mind that they are potential victims of more severe forms and action should be taken to counteract the condition in its infancy.

In rheumatoid arthritis the joints often appear swollen and red, and much pain is caused when they are moved.

In such conditions the actual joints must *not* be given massage, but good may be derived from effleurage and kneading *above* the affected parts.

Osteoarthritis also affects the joints, but in a different way. Heat and swelling may be absent, but there is much pain on movement, and in some cases there are crackling sounds of an ominous character.

Arthritis may, fortunately, subside for a time, and the experienced masseur is given the opportunity of rendering assistance in restoring the use of the joints, mainly by treatment of adjacent muscles, and it may be, by cautious movement of the joints, great care being taken not to cause fresh inflammation.

Arthritis is not a purely local disease but a systemic disorder and the consequence of many systemic disturbances. Most people fail to recognize them and if relief is to be obtained the patient should be encouraged to take measures to improve his general health, particularly from the point of view of nutrition.

The massage can assist greatly by attempting to correct such matters as constipation and improve circulation with appropriate techniques.

Much benefit may be derived from all that aids in raising and maintaining the vitality of the patient.

12

Treatment for Constipation

Many maladies, some of a most serious character, have been traced to poisonous matter in the bowels. And yet there are persons who, owing to pressure of work, or carelessness and indifference, fail to observe the rudimentary rule of health that calls for regular bowel movement.

There are, however, many persons who through no obvious fault of their own, are constipated.

For them constipation is a frustrating affliction with the tiresome need to resort to the use of purgatives, sometimes permanently. It is clearly preferable to stimulate the action of the bowels by more natural means, and massage has proved to be a most effective aid to the restoration of normal function.

The masseur will make sure that a considerable time has passed since the patient had a meal, and that the bladder has been emptied. Other necessary conditions are that there should be no inflammation or suspicion of ulcers, or a high temperature, and quite obviously no abdominal treatment should be given in pregnancy.

In all cases of doubt medical advice should be sought. There are, however, very many persons who may be given abdominal massage with safety and benefit.

It is found at times that even a little light treatment in the form of effleurage and gentle kneading has a good effect, particularly in cases of convalescence.

But in other cases the masseur will have to contend against remarkably stubborn conditions. These will, however, be overcome by the exercise of skill, and a daily renewal of the treatment.

In dealing with all cases, whether they are of a difficult character, requiring the service of an experienced masseur, or of a nature that allows relatives and friends to render 'first aid', the patient's knees should be raised and supported with a pillow.

Abdominal Massage

The operator's first aim should be to bring about complete relaxation of the abdominal muscles. Taking up a suitable position on the right-hand side of the patient, he will give gentle effleurage in a clockwise direction over the whole area of the abdomen.

Kneading movements, light at first but gradually becoming firmer and deeper, may follow. This treatment may be continued until the operator is satisfied that he has the soft tissues under his control. He will then give friction treatment, beginning at the lower left-hand side of the abdomen, and moving upwards, but with downward pressure, in small circles, treating one limited area after another in a manner that affects the underlying tissues and aids in moving obstructive matter.

Deep effleurage should follow, the firm sweep of the hand following the course of the former treatment. After repeating the movement several times, the operator will treat what is known as the transverse colon, and will then pass on to the ascending colon. In each case he will employ much the same movements.

Friction will also be given over the whole inner area of the abdomen, commencing in the centre and working in small circles in a clockwise direction, thus stimulating the small intestines.

Deep kneading will then again be given over the whole abdomen, and also shaking and 'cupping' treatment with the palms of the hands.

Experienced masseurs often use, considerable vigour, not only over the abdomen, but also over the area of the liver.

But the beginner is advised to exercise care and discretion. Unless he has knowledge of the organs with which he is dealing and experience of the actual effects of abdominal massage, he must avoid giving very forceful treatment.

Comparatively gentle massage may, in any case bring about the desired effect. Even stroking with the fingertips will cause beneficial contractions.

Constipation is often due to lack of exercise of the abdominal muscles from sedentary occupations. Even

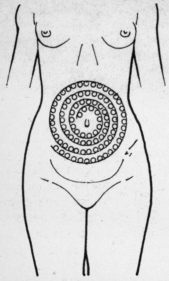

Direction of strokes for abdominal friction.

those who have jobs which involve walking and lifting may not use their abdominal muscles regularly. The result is that they lose muscle tone and the intestines become atonic. Such a condition may not only lead to constipation but also have a wide inducing effect upon general health.

It is not difficult to see that a considerable number of modern disorders arise from intoxication of the bloodstream and sluggish activity of the organs. Abdominal treatment is, therefore, very useful and can be employed with good effect in the treatment of most disorders. It should always be used when treating headaches, indigestion, stress conditions and arthritis.

13

Beauty Treatment

The cultivation of beauty has engaged the minds of women since time immemorial.

Massage is sometimes mentioned as an aid to beauty but the sort of massage generally given, which consists chiefly of friction, is of doubtful value. Massage, however, properly used may be a great aid to physical beauty. Not only has it the power to improve the condition of the skin, and consequently the complexion, but also to give litheness and grace to the whole physical form.

General massage should be given when possible, but the treatment will not of necessity follow the usual methods of giving the leading movements.

Effleurage combined with kneading may, however, form the main part of the treatment. The effleurage strokes will be long and fairly firm, and will be designed to mould the figure into lines of beauty.

Kneading will be given when there is the least indication of stiffness or undue firmness of the muscles, the aim being to remove all lumpy formations and mould the tissues into graceful lines.

Classical Beauty
The superb statues of ancient Greece show how graceful and lovely limbs can be when they form a 'unified rhythm' of line.

In our own day the ideal is illustrated by the rhythmic grace of classical dancers. Their limbs seem to 'flow' without the least effort. Such grace is the outcome of muscles entirely free from imperfections and perfectly attuned.

If the feminine form is to compare with classical beauty it must, be entirely free from the faintest suspicion of hard or lumpy formations. To soften hard tissues must, therefore, be the first aim of the masseur or the masseuse.

Effleurage must, if necessary, be followed by pétrissage, specially designed to remove imperfections. Patience and skill, will be required but the work can be done, and the figure under treatment may acquire more graceful lines.

The wrists, the ankles, and possibly the neck may be given suitable friction, and this may in certain cases be applied to the fingers and toes, and also the arch and instep of each foot.

The massage movements may be varied to suit the particular case, but the friction given to the head should in all cases be designed to move the scalp, and the tapotement that may follow should be given with the tips of the fingers so as to stimulate the flow of blood.

Gentle Friction

Gentle friction, causing the movement of the soft underlying tissues, may be given to the face, combined with gentle tapping with the tips of the fingers, followed by stroking movements designed to influence the flow of blood and lymph, and smooth out any threat of wrinkles.

Delicacy of touch will be required not only in treating the face, but also the whole of the body. There will, however, be times when gentleness must be combined with firmness.

It is assumed that the operator will have by nature the smooth hands and sensitive touch necessary for the work, and that a good talcum powder will be available.

Both hands may be employed in performing the various massage movements. There should be rhythm in the way the strokes follow one another and blend together. There should be no pause once the treatment has been commenced. The whole series of movements should constitute one unified effort, and the general effect should be soothing, pleasant and refreshing.

14

Aid for Athletes

Here again we are reminded of the statues of ancient Greece which have the appearance of a balanced but not overdeveloped musculature and give the impression of pliability of limbs. This kind of development can be taken as a model for those who hope to build up their bodies in such a way that power may be used with minimum effort. An athlete's muscles must not be hard or tight.

One may expect to see muscles 'like steel cords' in certain manual labourers. Their type of work often makes such a condition almost inevitable. But the athlete should be devoid of conditions that check perfect freedom of movement. If there is in any part of the figure hard or fibrous muscles, they must be treated. The whole of the tissues must be kept pliant and supple.

Effleurage in long firm strokes may open the treatment, but the main work will be with pétrissage, combined with much kneading.

The treatment may be fairly vigorous, but even young athletes have been known to complain when an over-ardent masseur has dealt, for example, with the abdomen as though it were made of rubber. Even when treating men who are used to the 'rough and tumble' of field games some restraint must be used.

It has been complained that certain men who aspire

to give massage treatment to members of athletic clubs
have little, or no knowledge, of scientific methods and
are inclined to 'rub' and 'pomble'.

Scientific Massage
Neither of the rough methods complained of have any
part in modern scientific massage. Ancient records tell
of 'rubbing', but we have left that primitive method
behind. There are no backward and forward
movements in modern massage. All the movements are
in one direction — towards the heart. There may be
exceptions in small or limited areas. But towards the
heart is the general rule.

As for what has been called 'pombling', that also is
crude and outdated. The aim in modern scientific
massage is to deal with individual muscles; not to
bring down indiscriminate force upon a mass
formation of tissues.

It has been said that to do the work of a masseur
without any knowledge of anatomy is to work in the
dark, and that, in a sense, is true. But fortunately the
would-be masseur has muscles of his own, bones of his
own, and internal organs of his own, from which he
may learn a great deal.

It is better, as stated, to know the position and
nature of muscles than simply to be acquainted with
their Latin names. *Know thyself* is an admirable
precept.

Effects of Fatigue
Massage is not only of value in keeping the body in fit
condition for vigorous physical exercises, but is also of
great value in removing the effects of fatigue, and
restoring the limbs and the whole physical frame to the
condition that permits of further effort.

In fatigue there are certain toxins — the outcome of

chemical changes—which should be cleared from the bloodstream. This may be done so well by the right kind of massage that a few moments of treatment will restore energy more effectively than a very much longer period of rest.

The treatment mainly consists of effleurage in the form of long firm strokes that have the effect of clearing away toxins, and renewing the flow of blood and lymph.

Other massage movements may follow, but effleurage is the cleanser and restorer that removes fatigue as if by magic.

Indeed, the masseur has at his command, not only the means for aiding exhausted athletes, but also the many other persons who, owing to the nature of their work or other causes, are often reduced to a state of extreme weariness. The treatment, however, should be lighter than for athletes, and should conclude with the kind of gentle soothing strokes that give a sense of well-being and refreshment.

15

Treatment after Injuries

The masseur who is engaged in building up and keeping in good condition the tissues of athletes will frequently be called upon to treat such injuries as sprains and strains, and, possibly, to render *first aid* in more serious conditions.

It is assumed that he has the knowledge needed for such work, and that he will know how to deal with conditions which would be beyond the power of the inexperienced masseur.

The reduction of a dislocation will, no doubt, be performed by a surgeon. Massage will be given later, and the treatment will mainly consist of very careful effleurage to the injured limb, with special attention to the areas above and below the injury.

By this means the pain will be eased and the swelling reduced. At a later stage, the effleurage strokes may be deeper, and may be combined with the forms of pétrissage, such as kneading, that aid in restoring the normal condition of the muscles.

Pain — a Danger Signal
If passive movements are given, care must be taken not to cause acute pain. Indeed, pain must be taken as a danger signal. It should, however, be possible to progress slowly and patiently in aiding in the restoration of the normal functioning of the joint.

The masseur's part in treating a fracture will again be postponed until after the attendance of a surgeon, who will, no doubt, give definite instructions. Early massage treatment is not always possible; but there is much to be said in favour of early treatment by an operator who knows how to reduce inflammation, and keep an injured limb in a reasonably healthy condition.

In dealing with such lesser injuries as strains and sprains, the masseur will be guided by his knowledge of *first aid*.

A strain may be simply the result of an undue stretching of the tissue around a muscle, or to definite injury to the muscle itself. In either case there will be pain, accompanied by tenderness and, possibly, considerable stiffness.

Effleurage in the form of cautious stroking will aid in easing the pain and reducing inflammation. The alternative use of hot and cold water is an old-fashioned form of treatment, the sprain being first subjected to a flow of hot water and then of cold, thus alternatively dilating and contracting the blood vessels. It is possible by the use of massage to have a speedier and more beneficial effect on the blood vessels.

In dealing with a sprain the masseur is confronted with an abnormal condition of the tissues surrounding a joint, which may be caused by overstraining, and simply take the form of a wrench, or may be the outcome of tearing of a ligament. In the latter case the services of a surgeon may be required; for there is danger of synovitis, or other serious trouble.

The masseur may, however, play a useful part later, in treating the tissues above and below the injuries, and in rendering cautious aid in the restoration of the natural functioning of the joint.

Such treatment would be given having regard to any recommendations made by the surgeon. In all cases of injury it is necessary to use discretion and caution. Any masseur should endeavour, when and where possible, to restore the normal condition of muscles and joints. It is his duty to follow the instructions of the higher authority, and be content in performing a secondary but very important part in bringing about final and complete recovery.

16

Aid in Cases of Paralysis

Here we touch on a subject so wide that a number of stout volumes would be required to deal with it adequately so that we can only hope to deal very briefly and simply with some of the causes of paralysis and show how massage may be of help.

Broadly speaking, paralysis is the outcome of shock, disease or injury. Loss of motor power and sensation are among the main symptoms. Occasionally the effect of paralysis is loss of sensation without loss of motor power, while loss of muscular control may take place even whilst sensation continues to be normal, or only slightly affected.

The body may be paralysed vertically, from head to foot, or on one side only. The side of the brain which is affected is opposite to the side which is paralysed in the patient's body.

The work of the masseur is directed mainly to the unaffected side of the body, so that it may not lose power as the result of the patient's inability to take exercise. The usual massage movements will be employed—effleurage, pétrissage, with kneading, and also tapotement.

Fortunately, there is a hope of partial, if not complete, recovery in some cases of paralysis. This should encourage the masseur to persevere in his work, and lead him to employ all available means in assisting the patient.

The exercise of considerable ingenuity and skill will be required; for sufferers from paralysis are not always able to take up the customary position of patients undergoing massage treatment. New ways and means may have to be devised by the operator. But good work has been done in difficult conditions, and may be done again.

Local Paralysis

Local paralysis may affect one hand or one foot, or one side of the face, or other parts of the body. In such cases the masseur will aim, no only in seeking to relieve the local trouble, but also at improving the general physical condition of the patient.

Injury of the ulnar nerve may cause paralysis of some of the fingers, or, possibly, loss of power of the interossei muscles. To give another example, injury to the radial nerve may cause wasting of the forearm and 'wrist drop'.

All serious nerve injuries may, possibly, be followed by local paralysis, and it will remain with the masseur to decide how he can best prevent the disability from affecting the other parts of the body, while at the same time doing all in his power to combat the direct consequences of the injury.

The doctor in attendance will, of course, have his own views with regard to the massage to be given, and it may be that he will advise treatment that will simply aim at maintaining, so far as may be possible, a good general physical condition.

Indeed, this, as we have seen, is the main work of the masseur; and in paralysis, as in other cases, it is, of course, advisable that he should be content to play his proper part.

His work will be to give careful attention to the muscles supplied by the injured nerve, and to treat, under medical direction, a whole limb, or, it may be, the whole body. The views of the medical man may differ from those of the masseur as to what is precisely the best treatment. But the masseur will be wise if he underestimates, rather than overestimates his own individual importance.

There may, however, be cases in which a masseur, or masseuse, of high qualifications and wide experience, will be able to convince the doctor that certain treatment would be beneficial.

In those distressing cases of paralysis, in which we see old friends almost helpless, we may, on medical advice, give beneficial treatment. Fortunately, little, if any, harm can be done by giving effleurage to a paralysed limb, and it may be that such gentle treatment will be a source of comfort; for the sympathetic touch of a human hand often has remarkable virtue.

Indeed, it may, possibly, be that treatment begun with no great hope will lead to the happy discovery that power may be revived in cases that appear to be beyond recovery.

17

Treatment for Lesser Nerve Troubles

It has been said that the nervous system may be compared to the telephone, and that in order to understand the working of the brain and nerves we may think of the brain as the telephone exchange and the nerves as the telephone wires and the muscles and the skin and also the will as the various telephones.

Certain parts of the brain are connected with movements of the body. Other parts are connected with sensation, and yet other parts with vision, speech, hearing, thinking, etc. These parts are connected by the nerves to the distant parts of the body with which they are concerned.

Sensory nerves convey impulses, or, so to speak, take messages to the brain; while motor nerves carry messages from the brain.

What is known as the 'sympathetic system' relates to the functions of the heart, lungs, and intestines, etc., which are regulated by this part of the nervous system.

The organs of special sense are the skin, nose, ears, eyes and tongue.

The central nervous system is composed of the brain, the spinal cord and the nerves. It is with this system that the masseur will be mainly concerned, and he will, no doubt, remember that the spinal nerves pass out between two vertebræ, and are distributed all over the body to joints, muscles, skin, viscera, etc.

Spinal Treatment

The spinal cord is, therefore, the main source of opportunity for the masseur. Indeed, some masseurs have raised spinal treatment to a fine art. The amateur can not, however, be expected to be an expert in manipulating the vertebræ, or in doing the kind of work which is thought, in certain quarters, to be of high curative value.

The amateur may, however, find consolation in knowing that there is a division of opinion with regard to the actual value of some spinal manipulations. But it is established beyond question that quite simple spinal treatment often has a beneficial effect in nerve cases.

The nervous system is so constituted that in many cases it may be as readily soothed as it is disturbed. Gentle effleurage along the full length of the spine, from the lumbar muscles to the nape of the neck, will often have a remarkable effect. The movement should be slow and should be repeated again and again in soothing rhythm.

The Sympathetic Hand

Here, then, is an outstanding example of how friend may help friend. In cases of 'nerviness' the sympathetic hand may sooth and relax. In a similar way, as we have seen, the precious gift of sleep may also be given to persons suffering from such disturbing conditions as nervous debility and hysteria.

In such cases a special degree of tact and sympathy may be required; but it is within the power of an understanding relation or friend so to soothe a sufferer that after treatment—or even during treatment—sleep comes to bring relief.

The cases that are spoken of as 'just nerves' are often the most difficult cases. Efforts on the part of a highly-imaginative sufferer to subdue nervousness by will-power are often futile; for in a contest between the imagination and the will, the former nearly always wins. The sufferer's main hope of relief is in switching the imagination on to some new track, and thus having something fresh to think about.

Massage, by giving fresh interest, may have the effect desired, and at the same time benefit the physical condition of sufferers. It will, in any case, make them feel that they are having what nervous cases usually desire—sympathetic treatment.

General massage may be given, with special attention to the spine. All the movements will be of a soothing character. The masseur should be perfectly calm and composed. There must be no fuss, no bother. The aim must be to convey a sense of quietude and ease.

18

Aid in Other Ailments

The intelligent would-be masseur will by now have a clear conception of the treatment required for simple physical ailments, and he will probably feel that he is able to deal with certain rather complicated conditions. Indeed, he may be a *healer* by nature, with keen insight and special gifts of curing.

Flat-foot

He will, however, value the experience of other *healers*, and appreciate their advice and suggestions in the treatment of such difficult conditions as *flat-foot*. Much has been written with regard to this disability, and a great deal, no doubt, remains to be written.

Here we must be content with dwelling on the broad outlines of treatment, and leave it to the ingenious operator to devise other ways and means, for it is a condition that offers remarkable opportunities for the exercise of resourcefulness and skill, not only as regards massage movements, but also exercises designed to have a beneficial effect upon the bones, joints and muscles of the feet.

In any case, the masseur will give deep friction to tender places in the soles of the feet, and press the tips of his fingers and also his thumbs into the muscles, and employ other means, such as pétrissage, with the view to softening the tissues and removing adhesions.

With the same end in view he will move all the joints of the feet, even at the risk of causing a little pain. In a young person, if given correctly, this should be distinctly beneficial. But vigorous treatment should *not* be given to an elderly person.

If there is any doubt a surgeon should be consulted; but the amateur may in most cases venture to give the massage treatment indicated, and to arrange exercises with the view to strengthening the arches of the feet, such as rising on the toes and going back on the heels in 'rocking' movements, etc.

The amateur may also render 'first-aid' in such conditions as 'writer's cramp', by giving fairly vigorous massage to the muscles of the arm and the shoulder, etc.

Brains in Hands

In each and every case the treatment should, of course, be given intelligently. Mere mechanical movements, done without care and consideration, will be of little, or no avail. Indeed, it has been remarked that a masseur or masseuse should have brains not only in their fingers but their whole hands.

So many and so varied are the illnesses and disablements which may afflict the human race that we cannot hope to name each one and indicate lines of treatment. But there is not, as we have seen, any need to do more than make clear the principles and purpose of massage. When these are understood the treatment for the various cases should be obvious.

Take, for example, such a condition as gout. Cautious massage may, possibly, be given locally; but general massage, that avoids the actual seat of pain, has been found to be more beneficial.

General massage may also be given with advantage in cases of anaemia and emaciation, and in convalescence following certain operations. But care must, as we have seen, be taken not to exhaust the patient. The aim will be to maintain, so far as may be possible, the general physical condition of the patient.

This is the chief motive—as we have seen in case after case — of the masseur or masseuse, and it is doubtful if there could be finer or more worthy work. Both amateur and professional may, therefore, be content in rendering this important and valuable service.

19

The Father of All Healing

Now, in conclusion, let us take a brief general view of our subject. In our opening chapter it is stated that massage is the manipulation of the soft tissues of the human form. The theories of massage are, scientific in character; but the actual application of the theories is an art, and this is the side of the subject with which we have been mainly concerned.

Many books and sources of study supply the knowledge on which the theories of massage are based, and the would-be masseur is advised to avail himself of all that tends to increase his knowledge of anatomy and physiology.

We have seen, however, that over and above such knowledge comes the actual application of the various massage movements, and those other ways and means which the skilful masseur may devise in the course of his work.

A 'Fine Art'

It is advisable, therefore, that he should think of his work as an art, even as a fine art, and that he should so develop his skill that he may heal where other methods of treatment have failed.

If he continues to develop his finer senses and sensitiveness of touch, he should eventually gain a dexterity that makes it possible to deal with hidden muscles as effectively as though they were visible to his sight.

The Beginner

The beginner should practise in many ways; first, in hand and finger exercises to gain flexibility, and then by applying the massage movements to his own body, where possible, or to the body of a friend. In time, he will gain the skill that will enable him to give the right degree of pressure, and he should eventually be able to use both hands with equal effect, and glide easily from movement to movement.

Not only will the main parts of his hands be used, but also the tips of his fingers, the 'ball' of his thumbs, and the 'heel' of his palms. His chief aim in general massage will, be to quicken the flow of blood and lymph and aid in the discharge of waste matter, improve the function of the skin, and increase nutrition.

We have learnt that massage was practised as far back as 400 BC, and that the great Hippocrates employed massage and manipulation in treating his patients. The methods then employed were, no doubt, crude compared to modern scientific methods. But it is interesting to note that the earliest healers appreciated the value of massage, and that it is not without good reason that massage is associated with the *Father of All Healing*.

France and Sweden

The development of both the science and the art of massage has been slow but sure. In comparatively recent years the French have played an important part, and to France we owe the names given to the leading massage movements.

We are also indebted to Sweden for valuable

developments not only in the treatment of muscles and joints, but also for physical exercises. What is known as Swedish Massage is held in high esteem and is widely practised. But it cannot be denied that many patients have found it too strenuous, particularly when it has been applied in strict accordance with set rules.

Highly sensitive, nervous patients quickly resent, as we have seen, any treatment that gives the impression of being mechanical, and lacking in sympathy and understanding.

Importance of Psychology

Indeed, it has been observed that the study of psychology should form a part of the training of a would-be masseur or masseuse. In any case, it is impossible to overstress the importance of exercising the nicest tact and discretion in treating not only convalescents and nerve cases, but patients of all kinds and conditions.

There are, however, cases in which Swedish methods may be employed with much benefit, and with sincere appreciation on the part of the patient. These are the cases which allow the operator the fullest scope for his skill in giving deep, far-reaching treatment.

In the course of such treatment it has been found by masseurs endued with special skill that conditions, which have failed to yield to other treatment, have been completely cured. Such operators are, in some cases, therapists with a genius for manipulating not only the soft tissues, but also joints.

This, then, is the high standard to which the masseur may hope to attain. But not for all is such rare distinction. Many would-be healers must be content if they are able to render simple, yet valuable, service to sick and ailing friends.

It may be that in the course of such helpful work dormant gifts of healing will be revealed, and the operator, with no claim to outstanding knowledge, may possibly find that he has the magical touch that can perform seeming miracles.

Important Note

When Massage Should Not Be Given

Readers will take into consideration the chief aim and purpose of massage, and will be guided in its application by their knowledge of their own bodies. They will realize, for example, that abdominal massage should not be given if there is any indication of inflammation or ulcers.

Massage should, in fact, be avoided in all inflammatory conditions, or in any marked increase of body temperature.

Other conditions which forbid the employment of massage are an abnormal state of the skin, and in all circulatory diseases, and in any abnormal state of the bladder or ureter; and also where there is any fear of haemorrhage.

In all cases of doubt the wisest and best course is to obtain the advice of a doctor.

Index